Rookie
National Parks™

Glacier
National Park

by Joanne Mattern

Content Consultant
National Park Service

Reading Consultant
Jeanne M. Clidas, Ph.D.
Reading Specialist

Children's Press®
An Imprint of Scholastic Inc.

Library of Congress Cataloging-in-Publication Data
Names: Mattern, Joanne, 1963- author.
Title: Glacier National Park/by Joanne Mattern.
Description: New York, NY: Children's Press, an imprint of Scholastic Inc.,
2018. | Series: Rookie national parks | Includes bibliographical references and
index.
Identifiers: LCCN 2017023158| ISBN 9780531231944 (library binding: alk.
paper) | ISBN 9780531230930 (pbk.: alk. paper)
Subjects: LCSH: Glacier National Park (Mont.)—Juvenile literature.
Classification: LCC F737.G5 M38 2018 | DDC 978.6/52—dc23
LC record available at https://lccn.loc.gov/2017023158

Produced by Spooky Cheetah Press
Design: Judith Christ-Lafond/Ed LoPresti Graphic Design

Published in 2018 by Children's Press, an imprint of Scholastic Inc.

Printed in Heshan, China 62

SCHOLASTIC, CHILDREN'S PRESS™, ROOKIE NATIONAL PARKS™, and
associated logos are trademarks and/or registered trademarks of Scholastic Inc.

1 2 3 4 5 6 7 8 9 10 R 27 26 25 24 23 22 21 20 19 18

Scholastic, Inc., 557 Broadway, New York, NY 10012

Photos ©: cover: stellalevi/iStockphoto; back cover: Mike Hill/Getty Images; cartoon
fox throughout: Bill Mayer; 1-2: PCRex/Shutterstock; 3: Pung/Shutterstock; 4-5: Jordan
Siemens/Getty Images; 6-7: Inge Johnsson/Alamy Images; 8-9: BGSmith/Shutterstock;
10 inset: FOR ALAN/Alamy Images; 10 background-11: john lambing/Alamy Images;
12 background: Steve Kaufman/Getty Images; 12 inset: John E Marriott/Getty Images;
14: Craig Moore/Media Bakery; 15: Pung/Shutterstock; 16 inset: Sumio Harada/age
fotostock; 16 background-17: Sumio Harada/Minden Pictures; 18 top: Mc Donald
Wildlife Ph/age fotostock; 18 bottom: Frisk/Alamy Images; 19: Sumio Harada/age
fotostock; 20 inset: Ryan Rombough/Media Bakery; 20-21 background: Danita Delimont
Stock/AWL Images; 21 inset: danikancil/Getty Images; 22 inset: Doug Marshall/Media
Bakery; 22 background-23: Laura Grier/robertharding/Newscom; 24-25 background:
Danita Delimont/Getty Images; 25 inset: Corey Rich/Aurora Photos; 26 top left:
withgod/iStockphoto; 26 top center: Dan Thornberg/Shutterstock; 26 top right: Mark
Raycroft/age fotostock; 26 bottom left: Lisay/iStockphoto; 26 bottom center: GlobalP/
iStockphoto; 26 bottom right: Dorling Kindersley/Getty Images; 27 top left: drlz4114/
iStockphoto; 27 top center: JosefPittner/Getty Images; 27 top right: MGJdeWit/
iStockphoto; 27 bottom left: JackF/iStockphoto; 27 bottom center: jhorrocks/iStockphoto;
27 bottom right: DEA/C.DANI/I.JESKE/Getty Images; 30 top left: photogal/Shutterstock;
30 top right: vkbhat/iStockphoto; 30 bottom left: George Ostertag/Alamy Images;
30 bottom right: CatLane/iStockphoto; 31 center top: elmvilla/iStockphoto; 31 center
bottom: Rayvin55/iStockphoto; 31 bottom: Danita Delimont/Alamy Images; 31 top:
Sumio Harada/Minden Pictures; 32: Ershov_Maks/iStockphoto.

Maps by Jim McMahon.

Table of Contents

I am Ranger Red Fox, your tour guide. Are you ready for an amazing adventure in Glacier?

Welcome to Glacier National Park!

Glacier is in Montana. It was made a **national park** in 1910. People visit national parks to explore nature.

There are many incredible things to see in this park. There are **glaciers**, of course! There are also big mountains and beautiful waterfalls.

United States

←Montana

Glacier
National Park

N W E S

A big mountain **ridge** runs through Glacier. It cuts the park into different parts. Because of the split, the park has two separate climates. Some parts are warm and wet. Others are very cold and dry.

Glacier National Park borders a park in Canada. Together they are called an International Peace Park.

Chief Mountain was one of the first mountains to appear on a map of the area.

Chief Mountain can be seen from 100 miles (161 kilometers) away!

Chapter 1

Mighty Mountains

There are 175 mountains in Glacier National Park. One is Chief Mountain. It is more than 9,000 feet (2,743 meters) tall. That is more than six times as tall as the Empire State Building! People enjoy hiking on this big mountain.

The view from Mt. Cleveland is incredible.

Mount Cleveland is the tallest mountain in Glacier. It is 10,448 feet (3,185 meters) tall.

Triple Divide Peak is another mountain range in the park. It is famous because the waters that rush down it flow into three different bodies of water.

There are more than 700 miles (1,127 kilometers) of hiking trails in Glacier.

Blackfoot Glacier is named for the Blackfeet Indians who live in the area.

This Blackfoot woman is wearing traditional clothing. She is competing in a fancy-dance competition.

Chapter 2

Water and Ice

There are 26 glaciers in this park. These large, thick blocks of ice are about 7,000 years old. Two of the largest are Harrison Glacier and Blackfoot Glacier. Like all of the glaciers in the park, though, they are getting smaller every year.

There are more than 700 lakes in Glacier National Park. And there are more than 200 waterfalls. Beaver Chief Falls is one of the tallest. And Swiftcurrent Falls is one of the prettiest.

Lake McDonald is the largest lake in the park. It is about as big as 175 football fields.

People enjoy boating and paddleboarding on Lake McDonald.

Swiftcurrent Falls flows into Swiftcurrent Lake.

A grizzly bear can be up to 8 feet (2.4 meters) tall!

A mountain goat's thick coat helps it stay warm in winter.

Chapter 3

Wild Places

Glacier is home to a variety of **ecosystems**. Many different animals live in these areas.

Grizzly bears, black bears, and wolves can be found in the forests. Elk and deer graze in the grassy fields. And mountain goats roam over Glacier's rocky ridges.

Many smaller animals and birds live in the park, too. Marmots, beavers, and foxes live in the forests and prairies.

Wolves can go two weeks without food.

Some birds, like the ptarmigan (**tar**-muh-guhn), live on the ground. Others, like the golden eagle, fly high above the park.

The ptarmigan's feathers turn white in winter.

Marmots are members of the squirrel family.

Glacier is too cold for most reptiles. Only the western painted turtle and two types of garter snake live here.

Cedar trees can grow taller than many buildings.

Huckleberries are a main food source for the park's grizzly bears.

Many different trees and flowers grow in Glacier. The western part of the park has many cedar forests. These big trees can be up to 6 feet (1.8 meters) wide. That is as wide as a grown-up is tall! The cedars block out the sun, so only moss and ferns grow on the forest floor.

In summer, wildflowers cover the ground.

Sweet huckleberries grow in the park.

Brave hikers can cross a cable bridge like this one.

Tour buses take visitors through the park.

Chapter 4

Stunning Sights

Many visitors to Glacier drive on Going-to-the-Sun Road. It crosses the middle of the park and passes near all the best sights in Glacier.

In addition to natural wonders, visitors can also see historical buildings as they travel within the park.

Imagine you could visit Glacier. What would you do there?

There are so many things to do and see in Glacier National Park. You can hike through fields or along glaciers and cliffs. You can drive past beautiful lakes and waterfalls. In Glacier, there is something amazing around every corner!

Cross-country skiing is a great way to explore Glacier in winter.

These are just some of the incredible animals that make their home in Glacier.

golden eagle

northern
pike

willow ptarmigan

bighorn sheep

great
horned owl

black bear

Wildlife by the Numbers

The park is home to about...

276 types of birds   **71** types of mammals

Mountain goats are the symbol of Glacier National Park.

elk

red fox

garter snake

mountain goat

grizzly bear

marmot

9 types of reptiles and amphibians

24 types of fish

Where Is Ranger Red Fox?

Oh no! Ranger Red Fox has lost his way in the park. But you can help. Use the map and the clues below to find him.

1. Ranger Red Fox started with a swim in the southwest part of Lake McDonald.

2. Then he walked northeast along Going-to-the-Sun Road.

3. Next, he walked through the woods to Grinnell Glacier.

4. Finally, he decided to head south to see about having a picnic with friends.

Help! Can you find me?

Glacier National Park

CANADA

Grinnell
Glacier

Saint
Mary Lake

Going-to-the-Sun Road

Logan Pass

Lake McDonald

MONTANA

U.S.
Area of map

Alaska and Hawaii are not drawn to
scale or placed in their proper places.

Compass Rose
North
West ◆ East
South

Can you guess which leaf belongs to which tree in Glacier? Read the clues to help you.

A.

1. Whitebark pine
Clue: This tree has long, sharp needles instead of leaves.

B.

2. Rocky Mountain maple
Clue: This tree's green leaves turn bright colors in fall.

3. Red cedar
Clue: The leaves of this tree are flat and feathery.

C.

4. Aspen
Clue: This tree's leaves are round at the bottom and pointed at the top.

D.

Answers: 1. C; 2. D; 3. A; 4. B

Glossary

ecosystems (**ee**-koh-sis-tuhms): all the living things in a place

glaciers (**glay**-shurz): huge blocks of slow-moving ice

national park (**nash**-uh-nuhl pahrk): area where the land and its animals are protected by the U.S. government

ridge (rij): long, narrow chain of mountains or hills

Index

Facts for Now

Visit this Scholastic Web site for more information
on Glacier National Park:
www.factsfornow.scholastic.com
Enter the keyword Glacier

About the Author

Joanne Mattern has written more than 250 books for children.
She likes writing about natural wonders because she loves to
learn about the amazing places on our planet and the animals
and plants that live there. Joanne grew up in New York State and
still lives there with her husband, four children, and several pets.

EddiE haRA 2004-2005

I is for Indonesia

Bilingual English and Indonesian

by Elizabeth Rush

Illustrations by Eddie haRA

ThingsAsian Kids

I is for Indonesia

By Elizabeth Rush

Illustrations by EddiE haRA

I untuk Indonesia

Oleh Elizabeth Rush

Ilustrasi oleh EddiE haRA

Diterjemahkan oleh Refa Koetin

Dwibahasa Inggris dan Indonesia

Translation by Refa Koetin
Book Design by Janet McKelpin

For information regarding
permissions, write to:
ThingsAsian Press
3230 Scott Street
San Francisco, California 94123 USA
info@thingsasianpress.com
www.thingsasianpress.com
thingsasiankids.thingsasian.com

Printed in Hong Kong
ISBN 13: 978-1-934159-41-5
ISBN 10: 1-934159-41-7

Once upon a time in a land not so far away*...

Pada suatu hari di tempat yang tidak terlalu jauh*...

*(Florida)

There lived a young, bored bat named Bruno Alfonzo III.

Hiduplah seekor kelelawar muda yang se-dang kebosanan bernama Bruno Alfonzo III.

Every day in
Bruno's short life
was the same.

Wake Up.
Go to School.
Play (a little.)
Homework (uggg.)

Purple polka dot
pajamas and
back to bed.

Setiap hari dalam
kehidupan Bruno
yang pendek berisi
hal yang sama.

Bangun pagi.
Pergi ke sekolah.
Bermain (sedikit.)
Pekerjaan rumah
(uhhh.)

Mengenakan
piyama polka dot
ungu dan kembali
ke tempat tidur.

Bruno was feeling blue. So Bruno did what
he always did when he needed time to think.
Bruno walked down to the sea.

Bruno merasa tidak bahagia. Maka Bruno
melakukan sesuatu yang selalu dilakukan-
nya bila sedang memerlukan waktu untuk
berpikir. Bruno berjalan-jalan ke laut.

Something in the distance moved.

Ada sesuatu yang bergerak di kejauhan.

One tentacle
appeared.
Then two.
Then four.
Then eight.

"Hello," said
the octopus.

"Go away,"
said Bruno.

Satu tentakel
muncul.
Lalu dua.
Lalu empat.
Lalu delapan.

"Halo," kata
si gurita.

"Pergi sana,"
kata Bruno.

"Oh yeah. Where?"

Agus placed a suction cup on Bruno's wing and said in a very wise voice, "The world is big and round and full of adventures. Let's go to..."

"Keluh kesahmu umum terjadi," kata si che-
palopoda yang matanya berkilau. "Kamu han-

GO!

said a little beach critter.

"Ayo pergi," cicit si makhluk laut kecil.

Bruno jumped into the sea.

Bruno melompat ke dalam laut.

Sometimes the waves were wild but Bruno and Agus swam on.

Kadangkala ombak menderu kencang tapi Bruno dan Agus terus berenang.

They saw weird fishes and waxed philosophic about the meaning of life.

Mereka melihat ikan-ikan aneh dan filsafat yang berkembang tentang arti kehidupan.

Where do parrots
go in a monsoon?

And why do clouds
occasionally cry?

Ke mana burung beo
pergi saat muson?

Dan mengapa kadang-
kadang awan menangis?

Days passed.

Hari-hari berlalu.

All of a sudden a
big beast rose out
of the sea.

"Looking for wonder?
For mysteries and
thunder? Swim on
you adventurers.
Indonesia is near."

Tiba-tiba seekor
makhluk yang besar
muncul dari laut.

"Mencari keajaiban?
Mencari misteri
dan geledek? Ter-
uslah berenang,
petualang. Indone-
sia sudah dekat."

A striped
tapir lounged
on the shore.

"Selamat,"
the tapir
hissed.

"That means
hello," Agus
said.

Seekor tapir
belang-belang
sedang ber-
santai di
tepi pantai.

"Selamat,"
si tapir
mendesis.

"Itu arti-
nya halo,"
kata Agus.

The air was warm.
The palm trees swayed.
Bruno heard whimsical,
watery sounds.

"Am I dreaming?"
Bruno wondered.

Udaranya terasa hangat.
Pepohonan palem bergoyang.
Bruno mendengar suara-suara
desiran air yang menyenangkan.

"Apakah aku bermimpi?"
Bruno bertanya-tanya.

"No," Agus said. "You are in Indonesia now, and that, my friend, is Gamelan music."

"Gama-what?"

Agus laughed. The music played on. **"Follow that noise!"** he called over his shoulder.

"Tidak," kata Agus. "Sekarang kamu ada di Indonesia, dan itu, temanku, adalah musik Gamelan."

"Game-apa?"

Agus tertawa. Musik tersebut terus terdengar. **"Ikuti suara itu!"** katanya sambil menoleh.

Bruno and Agus swam from Aceh (where the trees are as big as school buses) to Java (like the coffee) and down to Bali to bask in the sun.

There are more than 17,000 islands in Indonesia. Imagine that!

Bruno dan Agus bere-
nang dari Aceh (dimana
ukuran pepohonannya
sebesar bus sekolah) ke
Jawa (seperti nama kopi)
dan terus ke Bali untuk
mandi sinar matahari.

Ada lebih dari 17,000
pulau di Indonesia.
Coba bayangkan!

In Moluccas they hunted
the blue-feathered casso-
wary, the deadliest bird in
the world.

"What's a cassowary look
like anyways?"

"I don't know," Agus said
softly. "No one has ever
lived to tell the tale."

Di Maluku mereka mem-
buru kasuari berbulu biru,
burung paling mematikan
di seluruh dunia.

"Memangnya seperti
apa rupa kasuari?"

"Aku tidak tahu," kata
Agus dengan lembut.
"Tidak ada yang pernah
kembali dengan selamat
untuk menceritakannya."

People in Indonesia wear crazy colored clothes called batik. And they whisper sweet nothings to Buta Kala monsters. Buta Kala monsters are the biggest and brightest monsters on earth.

Orang-orang di Indonesia mengenakan pakaian dengan warna-warni yang beragam yang dinamakan batik. Dan mereka membisik-kan kata-kata manis kepada monster Buta Kala. Buta Kala adalah monster yang paling be-sar dan pintar di seluruh bumi.

Bruno stood right side up, he was so flipping excited.

"Kamu gila," Agus said. "You're crazy but I like you," which is just about the best compliment an octopus can give.

Bruno terus berdiri tegak. Dia benar-benar takjub.

"Kamu gila," kata Agus. "Kamu gila tapi aku suka padamu," dan itu adalah pujian terbaik yang bisa diberikan seekor gurita.

Bruno and Agus explored the
Borobudur temple.

"Borobudur is 1,300 years old,"
Agus explained. "It's a magical,
man-made, stone mountain, a
crazy cosmology, the epicenter
of the earth!"

Sometimes Agus sounds like he
knows everything about everything, which he kind of does.

Bruno dan Agus menjelajahi
kuil Borobudur.

"Borobudur berusia 1,300 tahun," kata
Agus menjelaskan. "Itu adalah gunung batu-
batuan buatan manusia yang ajaib, kosmologi
yang menakjubkan, episentrum muka bumi!"

Kadang sepertinya Agus mengetahui se-
galanya, dan tampaknya memang begitu.

They visited
Agus' family in
Cenderawashi Bay.

The place was packed.
Peg-leg pirates!
Squids, sunfish,
cuttlefish! Technicolor
dreamboats!

Mereka mengunjungi
keluarga Agus di
Teluk Cendrawasih.

Tempat itu sung-
guh ramai! Bajak
laut berkaki kayu!
Cumi-cumi, ikan mola-
mola, sotong! Perahu
berwarna-warni!

"Listen up," Agus' mother said, "Have you done your homework?"

"Dengar," kata ibu Agus, "Sudahkah kamu mengerjakan PR?"

Maybe Indonesia isn't so different from Florida, Bruno thought to himself.

Mungkin Indonesia tidak begitu berbeda dengan Florida, pikir Bruno.

In Jakarta, Bruno and Agus got stuck in traffic **FOREVER.**

There are 18 million people living in **Jakarta.** That is twice as many as **New York City,** and all of them are going someplace!

Ada 18 juta orang yang tinggal di **Jakarta.** Itu dua kali lebih banyak dari populasi Kota New York, dan mereka semua memiliki tujuan masing-masing!

EddiE haRA

II 2004

The air was thick with dust and smog.

Udaranya dipenuhi dengan debu dan asap.

Bruno felt crazy, Bruno felt ravey, Bruno wanted to jump back into the sea.

Bruno merasa gila, Bruno merasa bising, Bruno ingin melompat kembali ke laut.

Which is exactly what Bruno did.

Bruno was ready to go.

Itu yang dilakukan Bruno kemudian.

Bruno sudah siap untuk pergi.

Somehow swimming back always seems
faster than swimming out.

Entah kenapa, berenang pulang selalu terasa
lebih cepat daripada sewaktu berenang pergi.

Soon Bruno was home.

Tidak lama kemudian Bruno tiba di rumah.

Bruno looked around, maybe Florida was just as exciting and wonderful as Indonesia. The air was warm. The palm trees swayed. Bruno heard some far-away, watery sounds...

Bruno melihat sekeliling, mungkin Florida juga menarik dan indah sama seperti Indonesia. Udaranya hangat. Pepohonan palem berayun. Bruno mendengar suara desiran air di kejauhan...

As Agus headed out into open water,
he recited one of his favorite poems.

"And the end of all our exploring

Will be to arrive where we started

And know the place for the first time."

T.S. Eliot said that.

Seraya Agus menuju ke laut lepas, dia
mengucapkan salah satu puisi kesukannya.

"Lalu akhir semua penjelajahan kita

Adalah dengan tiba di tempat asal kita

Dan mengenali tempat tersebut untuk

pertama kalinya."

T.S. Eliot yang bilang begitu.

The End! Sekian!

Elizabeth Rush

Elizabeth Rush has collaborated with contemporary artists throughout South Asia for the better half of the last decade. At work on I is for Indonesia she deliriously drank coconut water while listening to gamelan music in imperial palaces. She traded bites of grilled pork and bits of insight with EddiE in many-a-lost alleyway. Elizabeth has written for a number of publications including Granta, Le Monde Diplomatique, Asian Geographic, Project Freerange, and Asian Art News. Her book, Still Lifes from a Vanishing City, a collection of photographs and essays on Yangon, Myanmar is forthcoming with the ThingsAsian Press. She currently calls Brooklyn home.

Elizabeth Rush telah bekerjasama dengan seniman kontemporer di seluruh Asia Selatan sejak lebih dari satu dekade terakhir. Seraya menulis I untuk Indonesia, beliau senang meminum air kelapa sambil mendengarkan musik gamelan dalam istana-istana kekaisaran. Beliau berbagi daging babi panggang dan bertukar wawasan dengan EddiE di gang-gang yang terlupakan. Elizabeth telah menulis untuk berbagai publikasi termasuk Granta, Le Monde Diplomatique, Asian Geographic, Project Freerange, dan Asian Art News. Bukunya, Still Lifes from a Vanishing City, kumpulan foto-foto dan essai tentang Yangon, Myanmar, akan segera diterbitkan oleh ThingsAsian Press. Beliau saat ini tinggal di Brooklyn.

EddiE haRA

EddiE haRA is a retired punk in love with under sea creatures. Yes, he is a little bit short and chubby. Yes, he is a major meat eater. Yes, he is one of the most active Indonesian artists of the 80's generation. And yes, his work has been collected widely from London to New York City, from Jakarta and Timbuktu (just kidding about Timbuktu.) For EddiE, creating art isn't just about making something new it's also soul therapy. EddiE's inspirations come mostly from children's drawings, underground comics, robotic toys, bold colorful designs on skate gear, modern graphics, primitive and folk art, rock and punk printed posters, TV news, sci-fi movies, graffiti, street art, and Mediterranean blue sky. EddiE stretches his time between both Basel and Yogyakarta.

EddiE haRA adalah pensiunan anak punk yang cinta pada makhluk-makhluk laut. Ya, beliau agak pendek dan gemuk. Ya, beliau sangat suka makan daging. Ya, dia adalah salah satu seniman Indonesia paling aktif dari generasi tahun 80-an. Dan ya, karyanya telah mendunia dari London hingga Kota New York, dari Jakarta hingga Timbuktu (hanya bergurau tentang Timbuktu.) Bagi EddiE, membuat karya seni bukan hanya berarti membuat sesuatu yang baru, tetapi itu juga adalah terapi jiwa. Inspirasi EddiE kebanyakan berasal dari hasil coretan anak-anak, komik-komik underground, mainan robot, desain warna-warni yang berani pada peralatan skate, grafik modern, kesenian daerah dan primitif, poster-poster punk dan rock, berita di TV, film-film fiksi ilmiah, grafiti, kesenian jalanan, dan langit biru Mediterania. EddiE membagi waktu untuk tinggal di Basel dan Yogyakarta.

THINGSASIAN PRESS *Experience Asia Through the Eyes of Travelers*

THINGSASIAN KIDS: A WORLD OF STORIES

To children, the world is a multitude of stories waiting to be told. From the moment they can ask "Why," their curiosity is unquenchable and travels beyond all borders. They long to know how other children live, what they eat, what games they play. They become lost in pictures of other countries and as they gaze, their imaginations take them there. Places they learn about become part of their internal landscape and remain there, long after they grow up.

Recognizing the amazing capacity to learn that exists in childhood, ThingsAsian Kids offers nourishment for young imaginations, accompanied by facts that feed young minds. Bilingual texts and vivid illustrations provide an enticing view of other languages, other cities, other parts of the globe. Children who discover ThingsAsian Kids books learn to explore differences and celebrate diversity, while the excitement of the world unfolds before them with every turn of the page.

A knowledge and an understanding of other nations and their cultures has never been as important as it is today. ThingsAsian Kids is dedicated to making books that will help children hold the farthest corners of the world in their hands, in their minds, and in their hearts.

thingsasiankids.thingsasian.com

Alphabetical World

B is for Bangkok
By Janet Brown;
Illustrations by
Likit Q Kittisakdinan
An English-Thai
Bilingual Book

H is for Hong Kong
A Primer in Pictures
By Tricia Morrissey;
Illustrations by Elizabeth Briel
An English-Chinese
Bilingual Book

T is for Tokyo
By Irene Akio
An English-Japanese
Bilingual Book

M is for Myanmar
By Elizabeth Rush;
Illustrations by
Khin Maung Myint
An English-Burmese
Bilingual Book